Knitting
For Beginners!

The Ultimate Guide to Learn How to Knit & Start Creating Beautiful Things (*With Pictures!*)

By Amy Taggart

© Copyright 2014

Disclaimer

The information provided in this book is designed to provide helpful information on the subjects discussed. The author's books are only meant to provide the reader with the basics knowledge of the topic in question, without any warranties regarding whether the reader will, or will not, be able to incorporate and apply all the information provided. Although the writer will make his best effort share her insights, the topic in question is a complex one, and each person needs a different timeframe to fully incorporate new information. Neither this book, nor any of the author's books constitute a promise that the reader will learn anything within a certain timeframe.

Dedicated to those who love going beyond their own frontiers.

Keep on pushing,

Amy Taggart

Table of Contents

Preview Of "Crochet For Beginners - The Ultimate Guide to Learn How to Crochet & Start Creating Beautiful Things (With Pictures!)"

Introduction

I want to thank you and congratulate you for downloading the book "Knitting For Beginners! - The Ultimate Guide to Learn How To Knit & Start Creating Beautiful Things (With Pictures!).

This book contains everything you need for you to pick up a pair of knitting needles and learn the basics of how to knit. It even explores some of the more advanced stitches as well as a few tips for making your knitting life a bit easier.

Firstly, let me say that there are an infinite number of sites, books, videos and downloadable material out there which you could try for learning how to knit – however, not all of them are as clear and understandable as they claim to be.

It could be that you have tried one or more of them and the reason you are purchasing this book is that those methods haven't worked for you.

We all find that our spare time is precious enough without having to research for hours on finding the easiest tutorial for learning a particular aspect of a new craft. This book will endeavor to make the time and energy you do spend more pleasurable by being able to produce something which your family and friends will love.

Did you know, for instance, that making the cast-on row can also include your first main row at the same time? Or that the inner circle you need to make some plush toys can be made as small as you could possibly want.

The tricks and tips contained within this book are set up in such a way that you don't need to read the entire book in one sitting – you can pick and choose which methods you use. If you already have some experience in knitting but want to refresh your memory or simply want to learn a new stitching method, this book can help.

So, pick up those knitting needles, grab your favorite yarn and start the journey with me.

Ready to create beautiful things?

Let's get started!

Lesson #1 – Welcome To The Amazing World of Knitting!

Before we immerse ourselves in learning the different types of stitches and how to read patterns, let's look at some of the topics which will help you secure a solid foundation when it comes to learning how to knit:

- What is knitting?
- Types of yarn
- Yarn labeling
- Needle types
- Needle sizes
- Left-handed
- Grip types

What is knitting?

For hundreds of years, people have become confused over what knitting is and what crochet is – interchanging the terms easily. To clarify, knitting normally involves two or more pointed needles (crochet usually involves one hooked needle).

The fabric made from knitting consists of working rows in stitches (usually knit or purl or a combination of the two for more advanced stitching). The stitches being worked are transferred from one needle to the other so that you always have an active row of stitches. This creates a tight, woven texture although with larger knitting needles, you can end up with quite a loose, woven texture if so desired.

Knitting can be done by machine but for the purposes of this book, we will be discussing hand-knitting as that is where the true skill lies. By using a variety of yarns and needle sizes, you can create anything from bags to blankets, from flowers to fun toys!

The word "knit" comes from German ("knütten" – meaning knot) and Old English origins ("cnyttan" – meaning to tie). From Middle English, it progressed to "knitte". It involves the process of pulling up loops onto the active needle and creating wefts, warps and wales.

- **Weft knitting** – wefts are created where each loop is perpendicular to the rows being worked

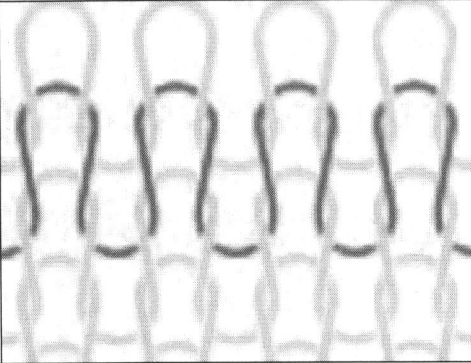

- **Warp knitting** – warps are created where each loop runs in a zigzag nature across the item being knitted

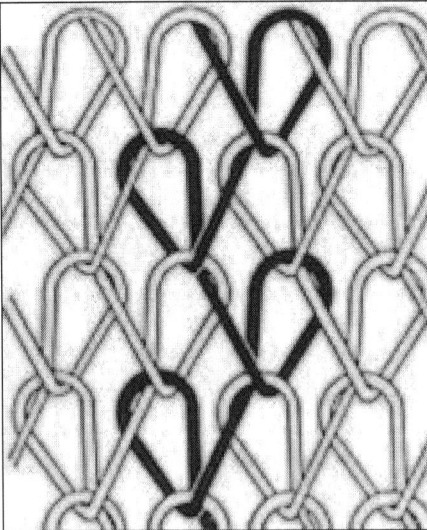

- **Wales** – a wale is created by the vertical loops made (for instance each red and white vertical row below is a wale)

Both knitting and crochet have gone in and out of fashion over the centuries; however, at the time of writing this book, knitting is now vogue once again and a wealth of material, information and patterns can be found wherever you look.

Types of yarn

There are several different types of yarn which can be used when knitting and the type you choose will normally be in direct relation to the type of item you are creating. Several of these types will be discussed in more detail in the following subsections such as double knit, worsted weight and baby yarn.

You will also find types of yarn which won't be covered in this book, but as your knowledge and skill increases, you can try your hand at. These include yarn such as coned yarn, kitchen cotton and eyelash yarn as well as specialty varieties such as ruffle or lace yarn.

Labeling systems on yarn packaging has been created by the Craft Yarn Council to ensure uniformity to the yarn being supplied to the crafter. Please note that not all manufacturers use this system; however, the vast majority does.

The main thing to remember is to practice with a smooth yarn which works through your fingers easily. This is imperative until you learn how to get the correct gauge and tension.

Double knit
Double knit yarn (also known as DK weight) is one of the most popular weights of yarn for knitting. It is ideal for light-weight projects and can be used for baby garments and blankets if it is soft enough.

It falls within the number '**3**' area of weighted yarns (or '**Light**') by the Craft Yarn Council – look for the following when purchasing DK yarn:

Some of the most popular brands of DK yarn include a portion of the LB Collection, Merino and Microspun.

Worsted weight
Worsted weight yarn is what is known as a yarn which is somewhat heavier than double knit (or DK) as well as yarns like

sport weight, fingering weight, and baby weight yarn. However, it is considered to be lighter than bulky or chunky yarn.

It is an ideal yarn for the creation of toys, accessories, clothing and afghans and blankets.

Labels for worsted weight yarn usually show the number '**4**' somewhere on the label to indicate that it is of medium weight. You may also see the word '**Medium**' on the label to confirm this:

Some of the most popular brands of worsted weight yarns include Bernat, Lion Brand, Coats and Clark, and Red Heart.

Baby Yarn
Baby yarn is one of the finest yarns you can buy and is perfect for creating baby garments, blankets and afghans (as its name implies).

It comes under both '**1**' and '**2**' area of weighted yarns by the Craft Yarn Council where '**1**' is known as '**Super Fine**' and '**2**' is known as '**Fine**' – look for the following when purchasing baby yarn:

Some of the most popular brands of baby yarns include a portion of the LB collection, Sock-Ease and Bonbons.

Yarn labeling

We have briefly touched on one portion of the yarn label but in order to know what you are working with when it comes to the various fibers available, here are a few more helpful tips about the information shown on your yarn label:

- **Care instructions** – this portion of the label will help you care for the finished product and how you should go about washing and drying the knitted piece. If you are using a very delicate yarn, you may need to opt for hand washing or dry cleaning to care for it.

- **Color name** – Each ball of yarn is given a name which normally closely refers to the color of the yarn itself.

- **Color / dye lot number** – Each ball of yarn should also have a number shown on the label which refers to its dye lot. A dye lot refers to the batch of yarn created when it was dyed. This is particularly useful when you run out of a color – you can use the combination of brand, name and dye lot number to order more. Be careful when ordering more yarn of a certain color as different dye lots can have result in slightly different shades.

- **Yarn ply** – This information will tell you the number of strands contained in the yarn (i.e. how many strands have been twisted together to make the single strand of yarn). You will see things like 2-ply, 4-ply or perhaps even 12-ply. Keep in mind that the ply number does not indicate weight or thickness of the yarn – it is possible to have a chunky 2-ply yarn and a very delicate 12-ply yarn.

- **Recommended needles** – many yarn labels will give you an indication of the size needles which is best suited to the yarn. By sticking to the suggestion given, you should be able to obtain the correct gauge.

- **Yardage** – The label will, more than likely, tell you how many yards of yarn are contained within any given ball. Make sure to pay attention to this as a chunky yarn will have less yardage than a fine baby yarn.

There are many other bits of information which can be shown on a yarn label, but you should at least have enough to get you started.

Needle types

When undertaking knitting for the first time, it can be useful to understand the different types of knitting needles available so that you know what to purchase to get started. We are going to look at the following types in more detail:

- Single-pointed needles
- Double-pointed needles
- Circular needles
- Cable stitch needles

Single-pointed needles

Single-pointed needles are the knitting needles used for the vast majority of creating knitted objects. They have a cap at one end (which stops stitches from dropping off) and a pointed tip at the other (used to transfer stitches from one needle to the other).

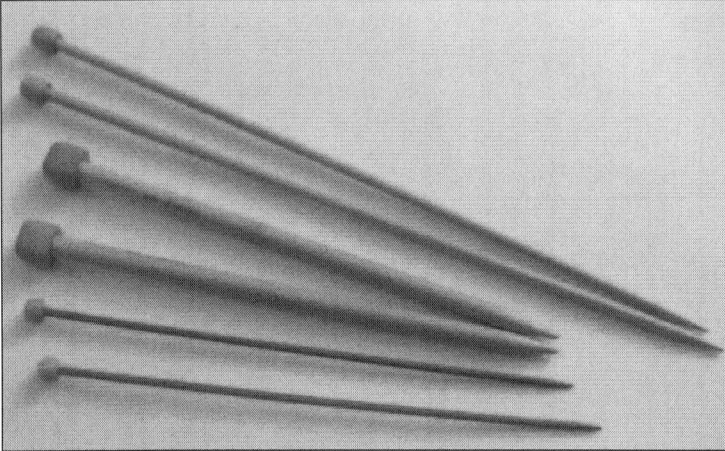

Double-pointed needles

In the early days of knitting, double-pointed knitting needles were used for creating circular garments such as mittens, jacket sleeves or socks – this is because you could get a seamless result. These are still used by traditionalists, but the vast majority of knitters have opted to use circular needles instead.

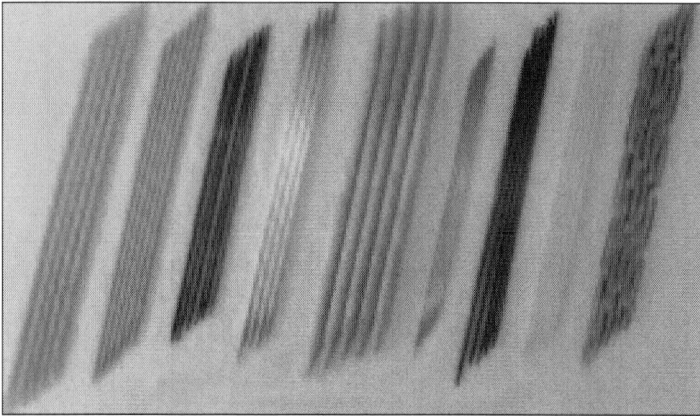

Circular needles

Even though the name suggests that circular needles should be manufactured in a circle, they are in fact only cord (usually nylon to hold its shape) with a knitting needle at each end.

Socks, mittens, sleeves and any other tube-type fabric can be made using circular knitting needles – even entire sweaters if the cord is long enough. They are also extremely useful for making afghans or blankets due to the length of the cords available.

You will also find that many knitters use this type of knitting needle as a great way of transporting items in progress as the stitches don't fall off easily.

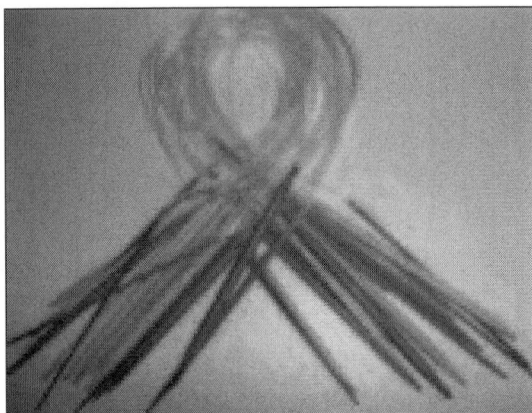

Cable stitch needles

Knitting needles used for making cable stitches have a curved middle section which allows the cable stitches to be held in place while working the remaining stitches either in front or in back of the ones being maneuvered to create the cable stitch.

Needle sizes

Knitting needles come in a wide range of sizes, and depending on where you live; you will need to understand that each country works with its own size style. The vast majority of patterns available come in either US or UK terminology, so a basic conversion chart has been supplied below:

Metric Sizes	US Sizes	UK Sizes
2.0 mm	0	14
2.25 mm	1	13
2.75 mm	2	12
3.0 mm	-	11
3.25 mm	3	10
3.5 mm	4	-
3.75 mm	5	9
4.0 mm	6	8
4.5 mm	7	7
5.0 mm	8	6
5.5 mm	9	5

Metric Sizes	US Sizes	UK Sizes
6.0 mm	10	4
6.5 mm	10 1/2	3
7.0 mm	-	2
7.5 mm	-	1
8.0 mm	11	0
9.0 mm	13	0
10.0 mm	15	0
12.0 mm	17	-
16.0 mm	19	-
19.0 mm	35	-
25.0 mm	50	-

For instance, if you live in the UK but your knitting pattern was written with a US audience in mind and the pattern asks you to use Size 6 knitting needles; you will need to purchase UK knitting needles in a Size 8 or 4.0mm.

Be sure to pay attention to this when picking up the various patterns available to you as the size of the finished item will vary greatly.

Lesson #2 – Gathering Supplies

As you gain knowledge, experience and yarn, you will soon find that you start accumulating other types of supplies in order to help you complete various projects. These can include:

- Blocking boards and pins
- Needle holders
- Needle protectors
- Patterns
- Stitch markers
- Tapestry needles

These extra supplies will be discussed briefly below.

Blocking boards and pins

For small items such as squares or garment pieces, you may find a need for a blocking board and a set of pins. Blocking boards normally come with a grid and a pin-through surface so that you can pin your knitted piece to the board to ensure even sizing amongst each piece.

Needle holders

Once you start building up your collection of knitting needles, you will need a way of storing them all.

However, if you want to indulge yourself, you could purchase specially made holders similar to the ones shown below:

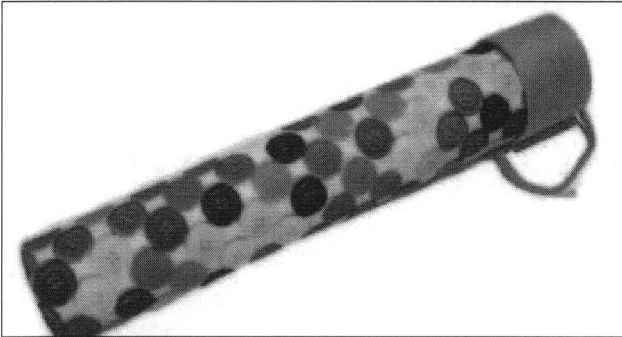

If you are a resourceful person, you could simply recycle an old can or paper towel roll tube for this purpose. If you have a woodworker in your life, maybe they can make you something like the one shown below:

Needle protectors

Knitting needle protectors are there to help you hold your stitches onto the needles when you aren't working on your project. For those who wish to purchase some of these, you could try the following:

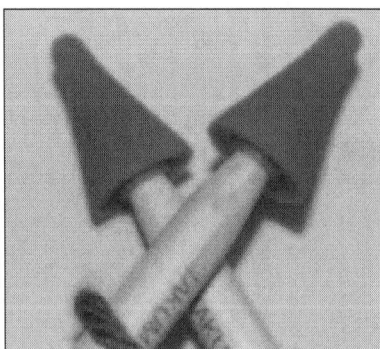

For those who wish to be resourceful, try putting a bit of silly putty on the end of your needles and remove when you are ready to resume knitting.

Patterns

You will find through the course of your knitting future that there is an absolute wealth of patterns available which can be purchased; and feel free to do so.

I would also suggest, however, that you use the internet as a fantastic source of material – a vast majority of the patterns out there are free to download; and if you have a laptop to hand or a cell phone which has internet capabilities, there is no need to print anything. You can simply save whatever you need as bookmarks and refer back to them later.

Stitch markers

Stitch markers are vital when it comes to changing color and leaving a color behind for picking up later. They can also be used for keeping track of a place in the design which could be difficult to find later when adding things like appliqués or the beginning or endings of a round or row.

Tapestry needles

Tapestry needles will become a very important part of your knitting supply collection because of their use in joining items together and for sewing the stray ends which are formed every time you change color or add a new ball of yarn.

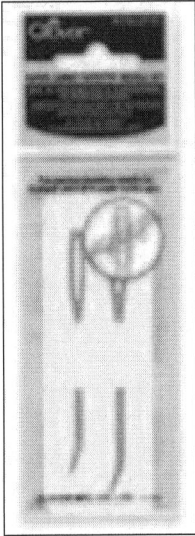

Lesson #3 – All Right, Let's Get Started!

Before we venture into the detail much further, let's learn about:

- Left-handed instructions
- How to grip your knitting needles
- How to hold the yarn
- How to make the slip knot

Left-handed instructions

Most of the instructions within this book (at least for the initial stages) will be shown with both right and left-handed instructions (with left being shown on the left of the page and right being shown on the right of the page).

How to grip your knitting needles

How you hold your knitting needles is entirely up to you; however, something similar to the images given below will help you to maintain the correct gauge and tension. You will also find that some people hold their needles freehand while others tuck the passive needle (the one taking the newly knitted stitches) under their arm for stability – the choice is yours.

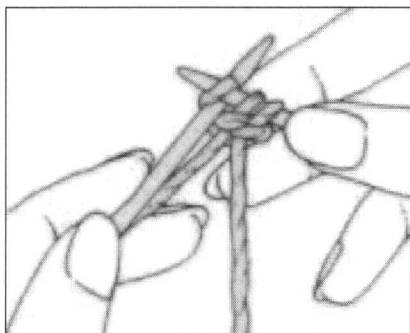

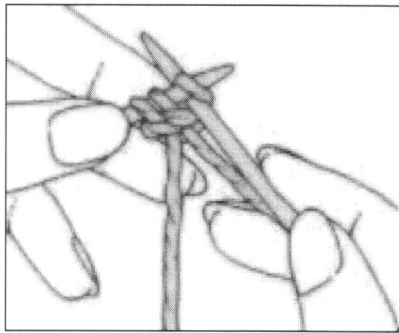

How to hold the yarn

Again, how you hold the yarn is up to you, but it is normally in the same hand as the hand holding the passive needle and works well if held over the forefinger.

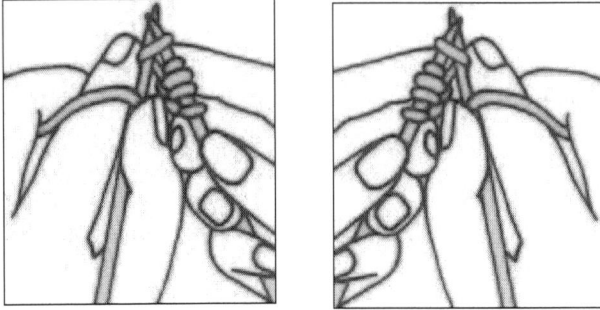

How to make the slip knot

Now we need to learn how to create a slip knot. There are many methods to this but the one we are going to look at is what I call the double-loop method. It does take practice, but keep at it – you will get there.

To do this, you need to put the yarn down and make the slip knot in the following manner:

- Using the tail end of the yarn, make an upside down U-shape and twist it towards the left to make a loop
- Using some of the working end of the yarn, do the same thing again
- Put the second loop inside the first loop, grab with your knitting needle and pull gently to tighten the slip knot

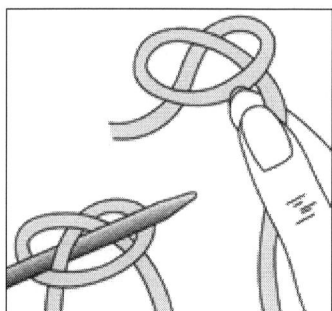

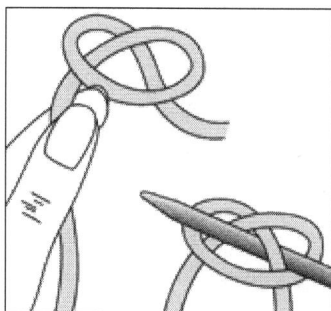

With the slip knot on one of the needles, practice picking up the yarn with your non-dominant hand and learn to hold both needles and yarn.

Once you are happy with creating slip knots and picking up the yarn to work, move on to the later sections in relation to abbreviations, pattern reading and stitches.

If you find that this method isn't working for you, keep experimenting out there until it feels right for YOU.

Lesson #4 – Flat Knitting vs. Circular Knitting

Knitting is done via one of two methods – either in the round (circular knitting) or row-by-row (flat knitting). This section will look at the differences in a bit more detail.

Flat Knitting

Knitting row by row is the norm and simply involves making an initial foundation row, turning your work, knitting each row in turn and working your way upwards – one row at a time. If, however, the item you wish to make is extremely large such as an afghan or blanket, then using a pair of circular knitting needles may make life a bit easier.

Flat knitting is a fantastic method to use for things like:

- Washcloths
- Knitting needle cases
- Garments
- Pillow covers
- Bags
- Scarves
- Afghans / blankets

Circular Knitting

The method of circular knitting is particularly useful if you wish to create items which resemble tubes such as socks or mittens. The original method for circular knitting involved using 3 or more knitting needles; however, as technology has advanced, so has circular knitting. Now, you can purchase knitting needles with cords attached so that this process becomes less cumbersome than ever before.

Try your hand at some of the following when you want to learn circular knitting:

- Mittens
- Socks
- Appliqué Flowers
- Christmas ornaments
- Hats
- Rugs
- Containers
- Bags
- Toys
- Placemats
- Booties

Using this method, you work with a totally different set of knitting needles which are joined together (alternatively you can work with three or more standard knitting needles to create the same effect). You then proceed onto the next row – either with the same color or by joining on a new color.

Notice from the examples which follow that 'in the round' does not always mean knitting in a circle – it simply means connecting the end of the row back with the beginning of the row:

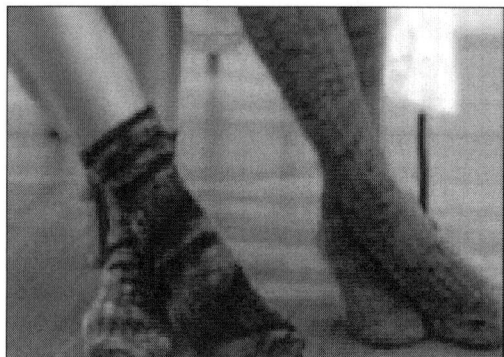

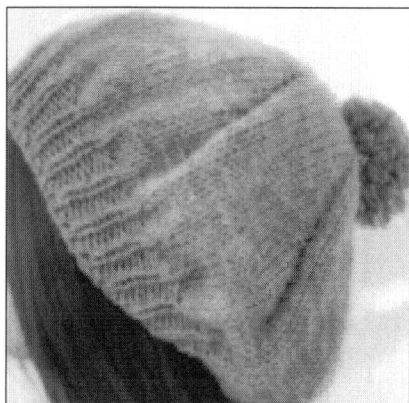

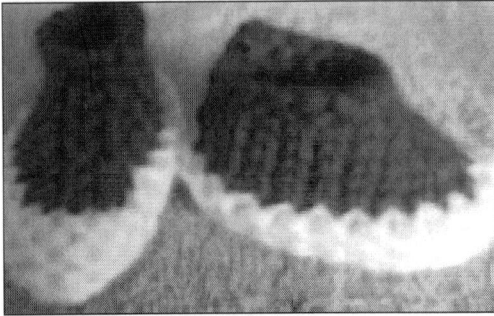

You can work 'in the round' in squares, triangles, circles or any other shape which works for you. Do bear in mind, however, that knitting in the round can also mean working in a spiral fashion.

Lesson #5 – Basic Stitches (With DETAILED Images!)

When it comes to knitting, there are really only eight basic stitches that you need to be aware of in order to create something of beauty. As your knowledge and ability advances, you can then move onto some of the more technically difficult stitches covered later in this book (which, by and large, are combinations of the stitches which follow).

For now, let's look at the following:

- Long-tail cast on (the preferred method and the only one covered here)
- Knit
- Garter
- Purl
- Stockinette
- Ribbing
- Slip Stitch
- Cast off (Bind off)

For the purposes of left vs. right-hand working, I will use the following terms:

- **"Holding needle"** for the needle which is held at the top of the work and holds the stitches from the previous row
- **"Working needle"** for the needle which creates the new stitch and holds that new stitch until you turn your work

Long-tail cast on

The usual method of casting on results in stitches that become quite tight and difficult for the novice knitter to work with. For this reason, I will be covering the long-tail cast on method which gives a neater edge and will result in a better tension for you to work with.

In addition, this method of casting on is particularly useful for creating the ribbing stitch as it aids you in getting the best elasticity for the garment to be made.

- The first thing you need to do is to think about how many stitches you need and measure out 1 inch of yarn for every stitch required (this length of yarn will be known as your *long tail*.   At this point, create a slip knot to place onto your needle (it doesn't matter which one as this method of casting on only uses one knitting needle).

- Hold the needle in your working hand (if you are right-handed, this will be your right-hand).

- Place the ball end of the yarn (not the *long tail* end) over and behind your first finger.

- Place the *long tail* end around and behind your thumb:

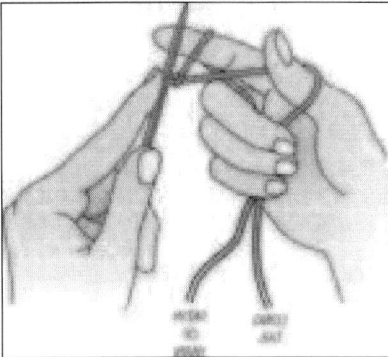

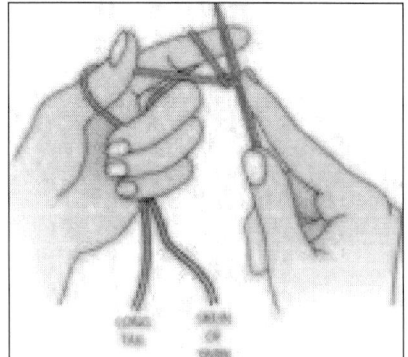

- Bring the needle downwards so that it is located in front of your thumb:

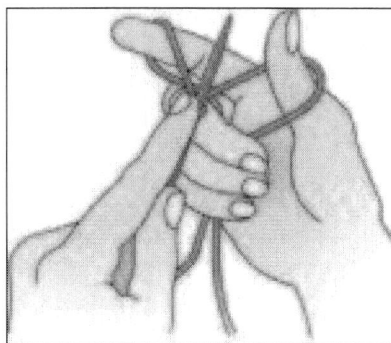

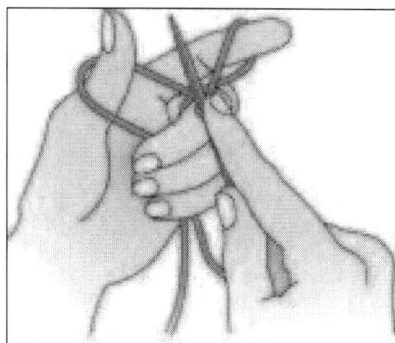

- Insert the point of the needle under the loop in front of your thumb (the bit of *long tail* yarn closest to you):

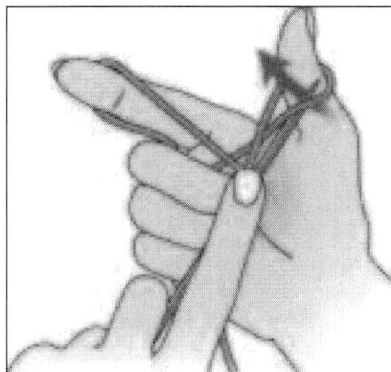

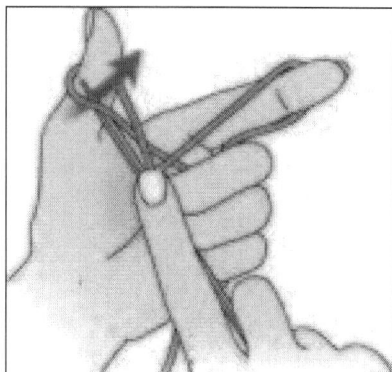

- Bring the tip of the needle up and through the loop as shown and then take the needle to the back of the other loop (the one around your first finger), go underneath that loop and up through the middle of it (you are basically making a Figure-8 with your actions):

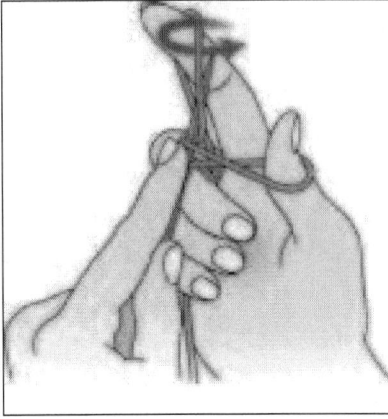

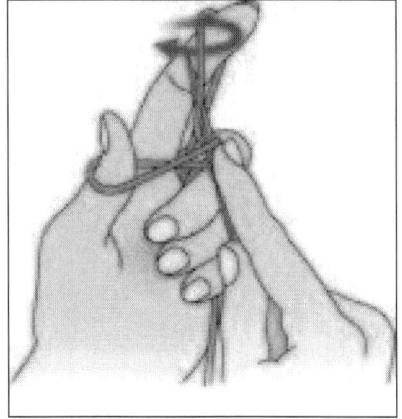

- Take the needle back through the thumb loop (but from the front this time) and pull it towards you while tightening up the cast-on stitch:

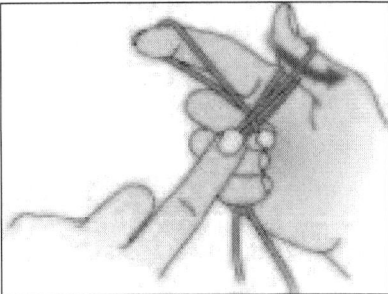

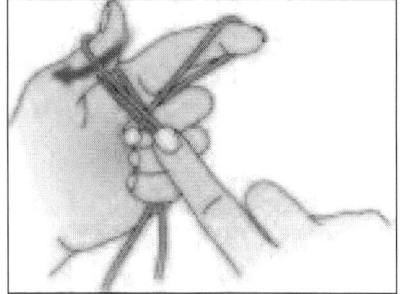

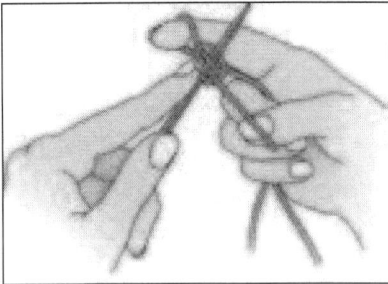

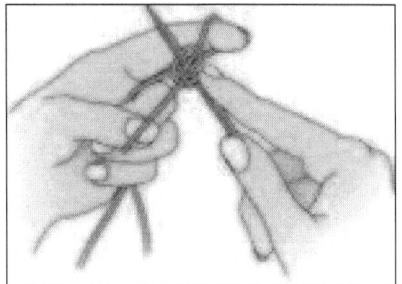

Repeat the above steps for each stitch to be cast on. If you find yourself struggling with this stitch, you will find that YouTube is an excellent source of assistance.

Keep practicing and, before you know it, you will be able to cast on extremely quickly using the long-tail method.

Knit (k)

The knit stitch is the most basic you will learn and involves working from the front of your work towards the back when picking up loops.

- Once you have cast on your required number of stitches, insert the **working needle** into the first stitch on the **holding needle** from front to back:

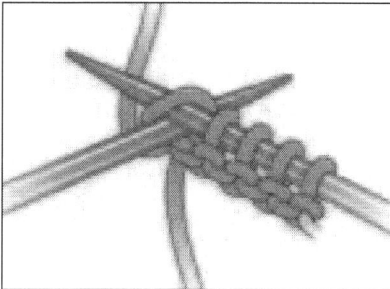

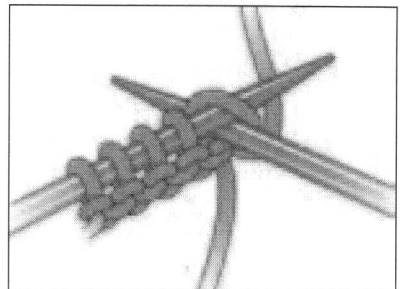

- Take the yarn and wrap it around the **working needle** working around the back of the **working needle** and around to the front of the **working needle**):

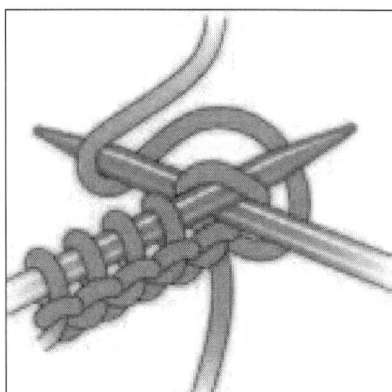

- Pull the yarn gently down so that the **working needle** can grasp it and pull the **working needle** down from the back and gently up to the front (while still holding onto that bit of yarn you've wrapped around it):

- Slide the stitch now formed off of the **holding needle** and onto the **working needle**:

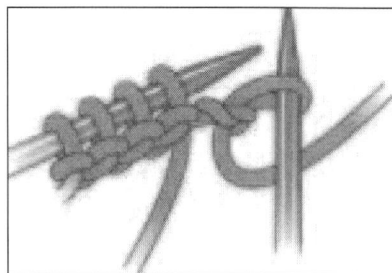

When all the stitches on the **holding needle** have been transferred onto the **working needle**, you can turn the work and start the next row.

Purl (p)

The purl stitch is done in the opposite direction to the knit stitch as follows:

- Once you have cast on your required number of stitches, insert the **working needle** into the first stitch on the **holding needle** from back to front:

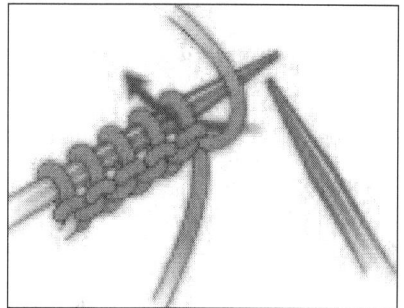

- Take the yarn and wrap it around the **working needle** working around the back of the **working needle** and around to the front of the **working needle**):

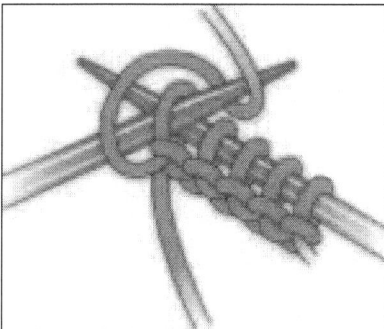

- Pull the yarn gently down so that the **working needle** can grasp it and pull the **working needle** down from the front and gently up to the back (while still holding onto that bit of yarn you've wrapped around it):

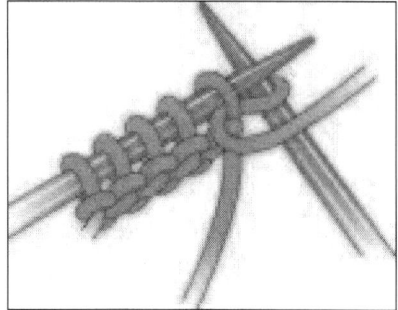

- Slide the stitch now formed off of the **holding needle** and onto the **working needle**:

When all the stitches on the **holding needle** have been transferred onto the **working needle**, you can turn the work and start the next row.

Garter

By using the knit stitch on every row (or the purl stitch on every row), you will create what is known as the garter stitch. This is considered to be the easiest knitting of all and produces fabric which looks like the following:

Stockinette (St st)

The stockinette stitch is created by knitting one row and then purling the next row (and repeat these two rows until you have the desired length). It looks like the following from the front of the work (basically all knit stitches) with each stitch looking like the letter "**V**":

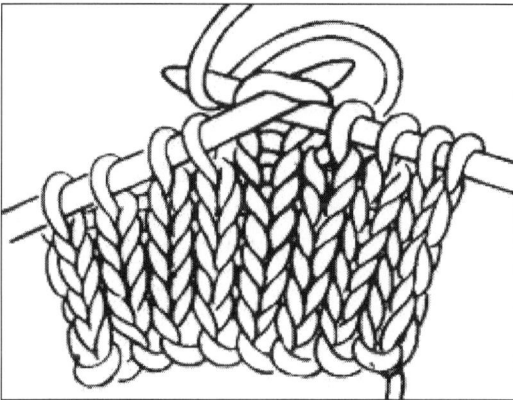

If you turn the work over, you will see that it looks like this from the back (basically all purl stitches):

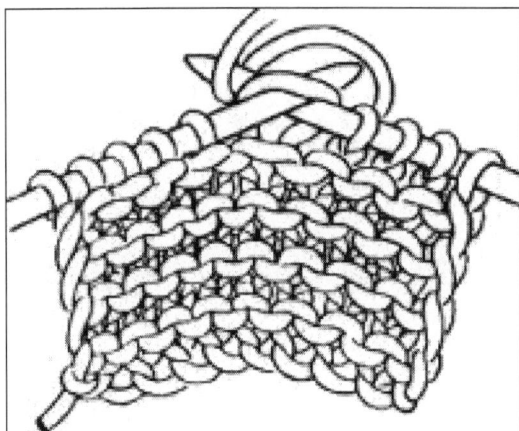

Ribbing

The ribbing portion of a garment is normally created for the purpose of elasticity such as on the bottom of a sweater or cardigan or the tops of socks.   It is created by using a K1 / P1 combination (occasionally you will find patterns that use K2 / P2 instead).

In order to switch between knit and purl stitches, you will need to ensure that your yarn is at the back of your **working needle** for knit stitches and at the front of your **working needle** for purl stitches:

- Knit one stitch by the method given previously with your yarn at the back of your **working needle**:

-

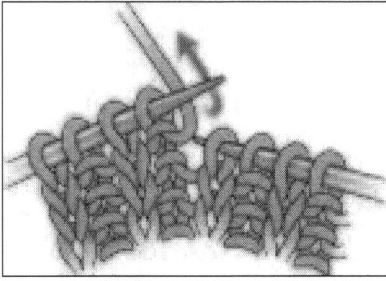

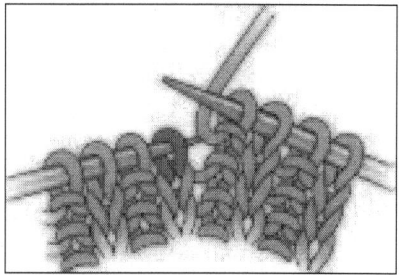

- Bring the yarn to the front of the **working needle** and purl one stitch by the method given previously:

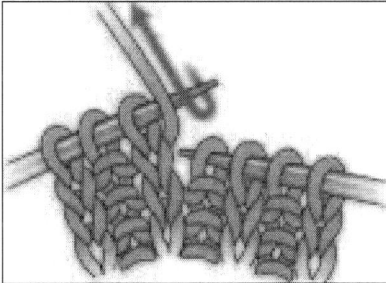

-

- Take the yarn to the back of the **working needle** and repeat the previous two steps:

Alternate Knit and Purl stitches until the row is finished (or for however many stitches the pattern specifies).

Pictures of both single ribbing (K1/P1) and double ribbing (K2/P2) are given below:

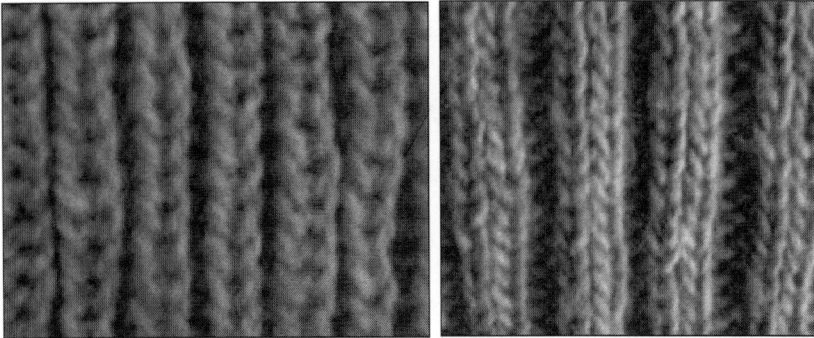

Slip Stitch (sl)

There will be many occasions throughout your knitting journey where it will be necessary to slip a stitch from the **holding needle** to the **working needle** without actually working any knit or purl stitches into it.

This normally happens when you need to shape the item you are making and when this occurs, it will be referred to as slipping the stitch knitwise (as if you were going to knit the stitch with the yarn at the back) or purlwise (as if you were going to purl the stitch with the yarn at the *back* – which is against the norm of a purl stitch).

- If you are slipping a stitch knitwise, insert the **working needle** into the next stitch on the **holding needle** as you would if you were going to knit the stitch and slip it onto the **working needle**:

When it comes to the point that a particular section of a garment is completed or you have finished the entire knitted piece, you need to secure the work you have done. This is done by casting (or binding) off.

In most instances, you will cast (or bind) off knitwise unless otherwise indicated by the pattern you are using.

1. Knit two stitches

2. Insert the tip of the holding needle into the first stitch knitted (on the working needle) and pull the stitch up and over the second knitted stitch and take it completely off the working needle.

3. Knit the next stitch and repeat Step 2.

4. When you reach the end, fasten the end off leaving a long tail of yarn to attach this piece to another (if required – such as a sleeve to the main body of a sweater).

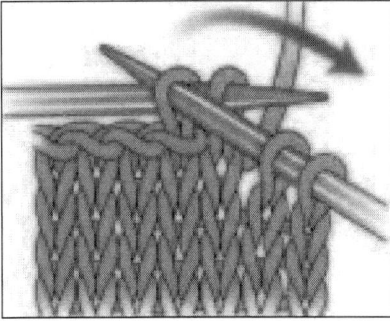

Lesson #6 – Reading Written Patterns

In order to condense the amount of paper consumed (or screen space if you are working directly from the internet or an Adobe pdf file), abbreviations have been created to limit the amount of words on a page.

There is a vast majority of abbreviations within knitting patterns; however, the most popular ones will be discussed here in an effort to clarify the meanings of what you see:

Square brackets [ ]

Square brackets indicate that you need to repeat the instructions which are enclosed within those brackets. For instance, you might see:

[k5, p2] 5 times

This literally means that you need to knit five stitches and then purl two stitches and repeat this four more times in order to achieve the 35 stitches resulting from this pattern).

It is also common for square brackets to be used when indicating finished sizes or the number of rows (or stitches) to be completed in relation to a finished size. For instance, you might see:

Ages 2 [4, 6, 8] – depending on the age of the child you are making the sweater for – that is what you will work to for the remainder of the pattern. Taken literally, if you were making a sweater for a 6-year old, then you would (for the remainder of the pattern), use the middle number within the square brackets for obtaining the correct size.

Rows 15-20 [21-24, 25-29, 30-34] – if we are using the same methodology as for the children's sweater above, then you would be working on rows 25-29 in order to obtain the correct sizing for a 6-year old.

Parentheses ( )

Soft brackets (or parentheses) are used to indicate where stitch groups are to be worked, such as:

(K1, P1, K1) in next stitch

This literally means that you would knit one stitch, purl one stitch and knit one more stitch into the same stitch on your **holding needle**.

They can also be used to indicate how many stitches you should have by the end of the row, such as:

(54 stitches)

This means that by the time you reach the final stitch on that row, you should have created 54 knitted stitches onto your **working needle**.

One final method for using parentheses will be to indicate which side of the finished piece you are working such as right side or wrong side. This can be seen as:

Row 5 (RS)
Row 22 (WS)

Single asterisk *

The single asterisk can be used to show that you need to repeat a certain set of instructions. This will normally be shown in a similar way as:

* (k1, p1) twice, k1; rep from *

This means that you would start the row with K1, P1, K1, P1, K1 and then repeat this set all the way to either the end of the row or until the next set of instructions.

Another example would be:

With A, p2; *with A, p9; with B, p1; with A, p10; repeat from * to last st; with A, p1.

With this pattern, you would be working with two colors (A & B), so:

1. With Color A, you would purl 2 stitches
2. With Color A, you would purl 9 stitches
3. Switch to Color B and purl 1 stitch
4. Switch back to Color A and purl 10 stitches
5. Repeat Steps 2 to 4 until you reach the last stitch and then, with Color A, purl 1 stitch

Approximately (approx)

This would normally be used to refer to gauge or tension and literally means that the result is not completely precise but pretty close to the desired result. For instance, you may see something like:

The finished afghan should be approx 36 inches wide

Beginning (beg)

A typical usage for this abbreviation could be something like:

Continue until piece measures 36 inches from beg

In this instance, beginning means from the foundation row.

Between (bet or btwn)

The term *'between'* is as it implies – between two stitches or between two rows – it means to work the next stitch between whatever is stated such as:

Change color bet second and third stitch

Contrasting color (CC)

Contrasting colors refer to any colors which are secondary to the main color. If you are working with more than two colors, then a different system will be used which will be more like Color A, Color B, etc. with a quick reference system provided at the beginning of the pattern.

If you are designing your own pattern, then use your own reference system but make sure you know which color is which.

Continue (cont)

This term is used quite frequently repeating patterns or stitches. For instance, you might see something like:

cont in patt for 10 inches
cont in patt until piece measures 36 inches from beg

This final one means that you need to continue in the given pattern until the piece measures 36 inches from the foundation row.

Main color (MC)

This will refer to the main (or most predominant) color in the pattern.

Pass knit stitch over (pkso)

When seen in knitting patterns, this means that you need to pass the last knit stitch over the stitch you have just worked.

Pass purl stitch over (ppso)

When seen in knitting patterns, this means that you need to pass the last purl stitch over the stitch you have just worked.

Pass slipped stitch over (psso)

This abbreviation means that once you created a slip stitch onto your **working needle**, you may be required to work one more stitch and then pass that slip stitch over the stitch just made (this can happen with any type of stitch). It can be seen in patterns as:

S1K, K1, PSSO, YFWD, P1

- This means that you would slip one stitch knitwise
- Knit one stitch
- Pass the slipped stitch over the knit stitch
- Bring the yarn forward to the front of the working needle
- Purl one stitch

A quick look at what a slipped stitch looks like is given below:

Pattern (pat or patt)

This is normally used to refer to the pattern being worked such as:

Work in patt until piece measures 36 inches

Remaining (rem)
This abbreviation refers to any remaining stitches, such as:

K into rem 5 stitches

Repeat (rep)

This term can be used to refer to both repeated patterns and repeated rows, such as:

Rep Rows 2-6 until piece measures 12 inches
*Rep from * 5 times*

Right side (RS)

RS refers to the right side of the piece being worked – this is the side which would be displayed or, if a garment, would be visible from the outside.

Round(s) (rnd or rnds)

If you are working in with circular knitting needles (for instance when creating socks or mittens), this abbreviation would normally be seen to indicate the number of rounds required, such as:

Work K in each rnd for 4 rnds

Slip one knitwise (S1K)

This is the same as a standard slip stitch and refers to the knit stitch to be slipped from the **holding needle** onto the **working needle**.

Slip one purlwise (S1P)

This is the same as a standard slip stitch; however, in this instance, it refers to the purl stitch to be slipped from the **holding needle** onto the **working needle**.

Wrong side (WS)

WS refers to the wrong side of the piece being worked – this is the side which would not normally be displayed or, if a garment, would be on the inside.

Yarn forward (yfw)

This simply means that you bring the yarn over your working needle into the front of the work. In effect, it allows you to add an extra stitch according to the pattern requirements.

Examples to further your pattern reading knowledge

Example 1 (and can be used to make a beautiful baby blanket with the yarn of your choice)

Using US Size 10 knitting needles, cast on 60 sts.
K10 rows
Work 70 rows in patt
K 10 rows
Cast off

Pattern

*Row 1: K5, *P10, K10 rep from * to last 5sts, K5*
*Row 2: K5, *K10, P10 rep from * to last 5sts, K5*
Repeat last two rows 4 times more.

*Row 11: K5, * K10, P10 rep from * to last 5sts, K5*
*Row 12: K5, *P10, K10, rep from * to last 5sts, K5*
Repeat last two rows 4 times more.

Repeat patt for 70 rows.

What this means to you is that you need to:

- Cast on 60 stitches using long-tail cast on method
- Knit 10 rows
- Using the "**Pattern**" complete 70 rows as follows:

  o On the 1st of these 70 rows (Row 1), knit 5 stitches, purl 10 and then knit 10 stitches (repeat this P10 and K10 until you reach the last 5 stitches on your row) and then knit 5 stitches.

  o On the 2nd of these 70 rows (Row 2), knit 5 stitches, knit 10 and then purl 10 stitches (repeat this K10 and P10 until you reach the last 5 stitches on your row) and then knit 5 stitches.

- Repeat the above two steps until you have completed 10 rows of the 70 to be done within the pattern.

- On the 11th of these 70 rows (Row 11), knit 5 stitches, knit 10 and then purl 10 stitches (repeat this K10 and P10 until you reach the last 5 stitches on your row) and then knit 5 stitches.

- On the 12th of these 70 rows (Row 12), knit 5 stitches, purl 10 and then knit 10 stitches (repeat this P10 and K10 until you reach the last 5 stitches on your row) and then knit 5 stitches.

- Repeat the above two steps until you have completed rows 11 to 20 of the 70 to be done within the pattern.

- Repeat the above pattern (rows 1 to 10 and rows 11 to 20) until you have 70 rows of pattern – this means that your pattern will finish with a Row 1 to 10 set).

- Knit an additional 10 rows.

- Cast off

You should end up with something which looks like:

Example 2

Rows 1, 3 and 5: (WS) P3, *k3, p3; rep from * across.
Rows 2, 4 and 6: Knit the knit sts and purl the purl sts as they face you.
Rows 7 –10: Knit.
Rows 11, 13 and 15: K3, *p3, k3; rep from * across.
Rows 12, 14 and 16: Knit the knit sts and purl the purl sts as they face you.
Rows 17 – 20: Knit.

This means that you need to:

- Work Rows 1, 3 and 5 (which is the wrong side of the finished piece) as follows:
  - Purl 3 stitches.

- o Then repeat a pattern of knit 3 stitches, purl 3 stitches until you reach the end of the row.

- Work Rows 2, 4 and 6 as follows:

  - o Wherever you see knit stitches (with the **holding needle** facing you while you work, they will look like V shapes), then knit those stitches.

  - o Wherever you see purl stitches (with the **holding needle** facing you while you work, they will look like raised bumps), then purl those stitches.

- Knit all stitches for Rows 7, 8, 9 and 10

- Work Rows 11, 13 and 15 (which is the wrong side of the finished piece) as follows:

  - o Knit 3 stitches.

  - o Then repeat a pattern of purl 3 stitches, knit 3 stitches until you reach the end of the row.

- Work Rows 12, 14 and 16 as follows:

  - o Wherever you see knit stitches (with the **holding needle** facing you while you work, they will look like V shapes), then knit those stitches.

  - o Wherever you see purl stitches (with the **holding needle** facing you while you work, they will look like raised bumps), then purl those stitches.

- Knit all stitches for Rows 17, 18, 19 and 20

Your finished work should look something like:

Lesson #7 – Increasing & Decreasing

Learning how to increase and/or decrease the number of stitches in the row you are working is paramount to successful sizing (especially in garments).

Let's look at each in turn.

Decrease

There are two main methods for creating decreases in your finished piece:

- On the edge
- Within the row

On the edge

If you are decreasing your stitches on the edge, then use the pass slipped stitch over (psso) technique.

Within the row

This is done by knitting (or purling stitches together) normally with:

- K2tog
- P2tog

K2tog

To knit two stitches together, insert your **working needle** into the second of the two stitches to be combined on the **holding needle** (from the front left of the 2nd stitch into the back right of the 1st stitch). This becomes a very tight stitch which angles to the right.

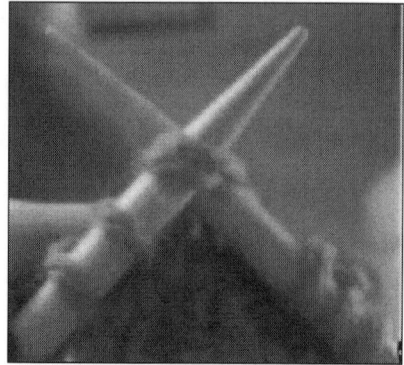

If you want to create a left-slant knit decrease, then knit the two stitches together by inserting the **working needle** into the front right of the 1st stitch on the **holding needle** and into the back left of the 2nd stitch on the **holding needle**:

P2tog

To purl two stitches together, insert your **working needle** into the first of the two stitches to be combined on the **holding needle** (from the front right of the 1st stitch into the back left of the 2nd stitch). This becomes a very tight stitch which angles to the right.

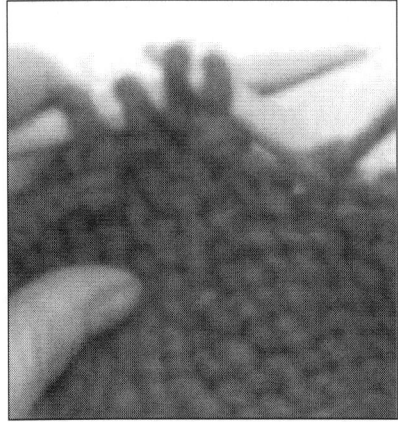

If you want to create a left-slant purl decrease, then purl the two stitches together by inserting the **working needle** into the front left of the 2nd stitch on the **holding needle** and into the back right of the 1st stitch on the **holding needle**:

Increasing

There are two main methods for creating increases in your finished piece:

- On the edge
- Within the row

On the edge

If you are increasing your stitches on the edge, then use the *Increase (inc)* stitch technique:

If you are working on a knit row, then you will need to knit into both the front and the back of the next stitch in order to increase your stitches by 1.

- To do this, knit into the stitch on the **holding needle** as normal and, before slipping it off of **the holding needle**, twist the **working needle** behind it and knit into the same stitch from the opposite direction.

- Finish the knit stitch as normal.

For purl rows, purl as normal into the front of the next stitch and then (before sliding it onto the **working needle**), purl into the back of the same stitch.

Within the row

If you are increasing the number of stitches in your row from within the row, then use the *Make 1 (M1)* technique. This is done by creating a new stitch from the loop between two stitches:

- Insert the working needle from front to back under the horizontal loop that lies between the stitch on the **working needle** and the stitch on the **holding needle**:

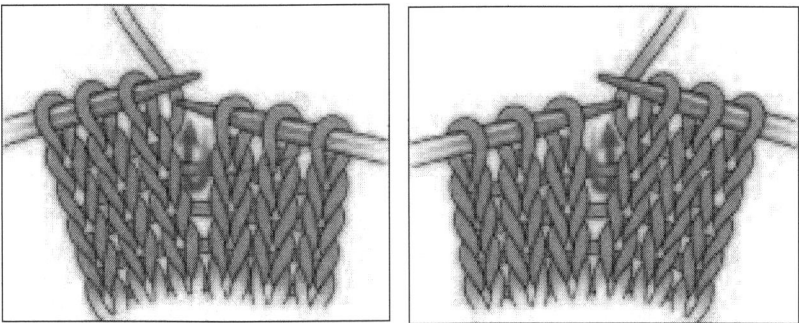

Pick this loop up and place it onto the **holding needle**.

- Insert the **working needle** into this picked-up loop as you normally would for a knit stitch:

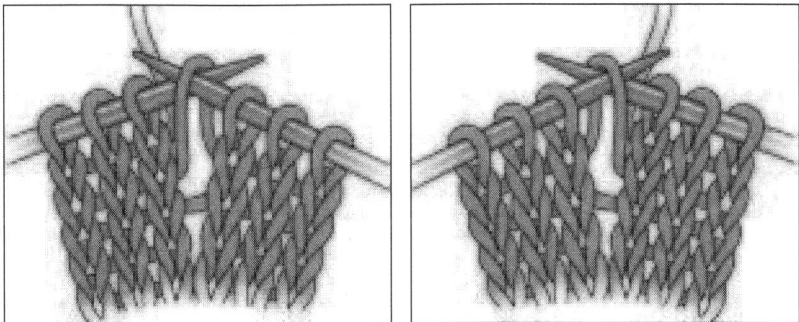

- Knit the stitch and slide the finished stitch onto the **working needle**:

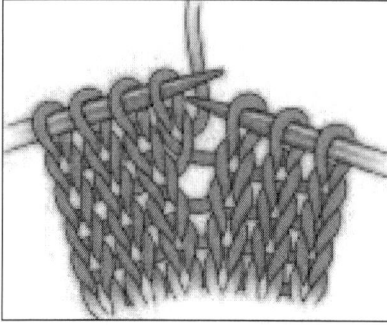

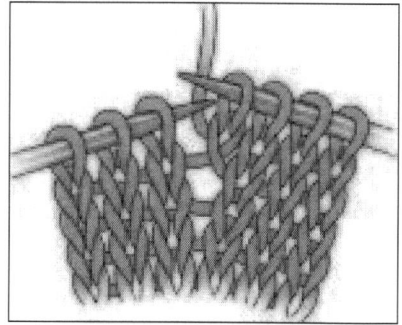

Lesson #8 – Changing Color & Fastening Off

Knitting is really easy if all you ever want to do is work with the same color. However, there are many occasions when you will want to change color to add variety and personality to your finished piece.

This section will look at how:

- you join a new color to your knitting
- you carry a color in your knitting

How to Join Yarn in Knitting

Joining yarn into your knitted item is relatively straight forward and can be necessary for the following reasons:

- You have come to the end of an existing ball of yarn and need to join a new ball in
- You want to change colors
- You want to add a separate element into the design

Regardless of the reasons for joining a new ball of yarn, the method is the same and is extremely important to learn in order to have your knitted item result in a professionally finished look.

Yes, it's easy to just knot the two ends together and carry on stitching; however, this produces a very unsightly finish. In addition, where possible, you should join the new ball of yarn into the end of the row. If that's not possible, keep your joins as neat as possible.

At the end of the row
To join a new ball of yarn (either same color or different color) at the end of a row, use the following method:

- Turn your work and join the new color of yarn with a loose knot onto the long tail of the old color

- Start the next row

- Once you have completed an inch or two of stitches, untie the loose knot and weave the yarn ends (both colors) into the row

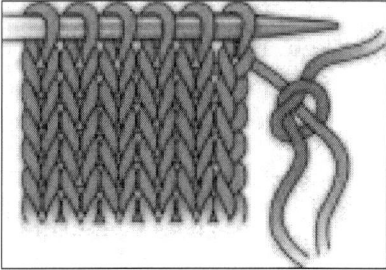

In the middle of the row

When you can't avoid joining a color at the beginning or end of a row, try the following:

- Stop working stitches when you have about 6 inches of yarn remaining from the original color

- Start working with the new color leaving about 6 inches of that color remaining as well

- Once you have completed several inches of stitches, weave each color into the work individually to secure

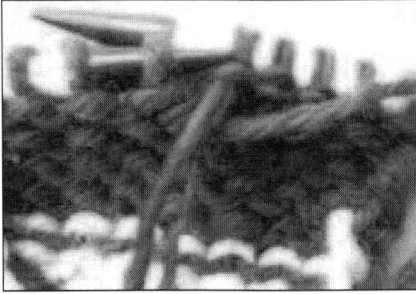

Carrying the yarn

With many patterns, color change happens frequently and, in instances like this, you will want to carry your old color with you until you need it again.

Carrying across the row

The method used for carrying the yarn is as follows:

- If you are working on the right side of your finished piece (this is usually the knit side), then hold the color to be carried along the back of the work and switch colors as necessary

- If you are working on the wrong side of your finished piece (this is usually the purl side), then hold the color to be carried along the front of the work and switch colors as necessary

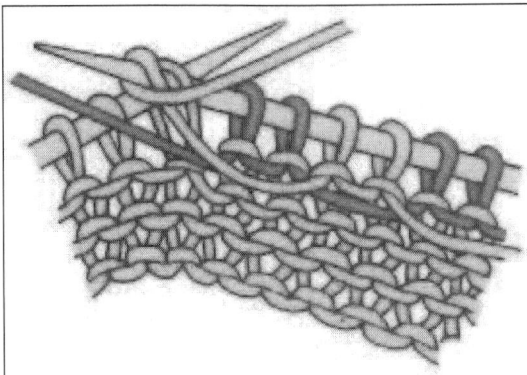

Carrying up the rows

This method is particularly useful if you are creating a striped item where two rows are worked of each color. The method given below ensures a neat chained edge along both sides of your work:

- Firstly, if you are going to carry the yarn up the rows, do not cut the yarn at each color change.

- On every row (on both the RS and WS of your work), slip the first stitch of the row knitwise (sl1k) and purl the last stitch of the row.

- If possible, make all of your color changes on the RS rows by picking up the new color from beneath the old color

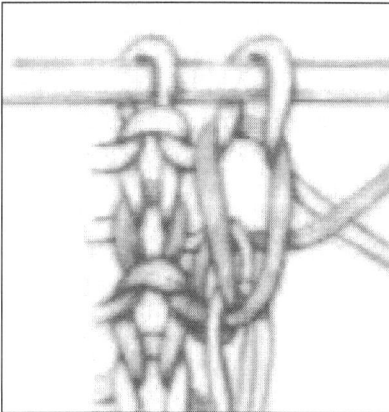

- It is important to ensure that these chains which are created are intentionally loose; otherwise, you will end up with a very tight edging to your knitted piece which will make it very uncooperative later.

- It is important to remember those slipped stitches mentioned above – they need to be incorporated back into your next stitch or you will end up with an ever-decreasing piece of fabric

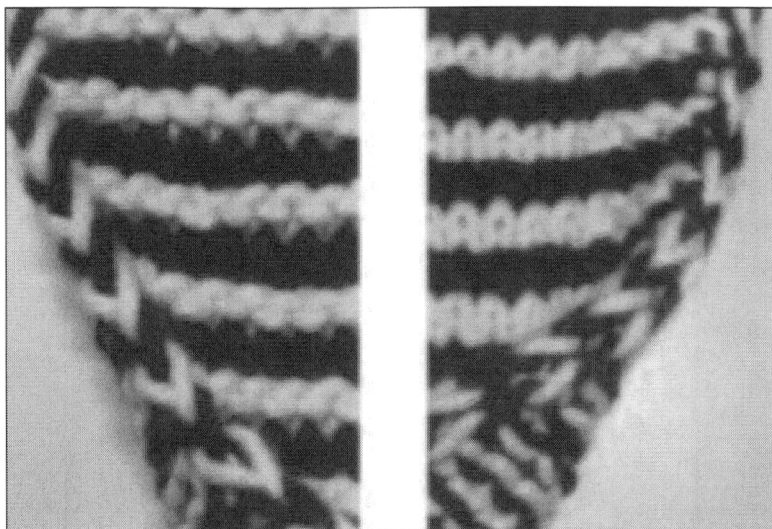

Lesson #9 – Tension, Gauge & Blocking

Tension and gauge are two of the most important topics in the world of knitting. Without fully understanding how to achieve either one of these, your finished pieces may come out in different sizes or the wrong size completely.

This is especially important when making garments. Let's look at these in a bit more detail.

Gauge

When we use the term 'gauge' in knitting, we are referring to the number of stitches and the number of rows you will need (per inch) for your finished piece to be the same size as what has been indicated in the pattern.

It is normal for gauge to be referred to in 4-inch blocks, but you may sometimes see it in 6-inch blocks instead. The pattern you are using should indicate the gauge clearly so that you can create a test block to ensure you are working to the correct gauge.

A good bit of advice here is to make your swatch two inches bigger (i.e. one inch larger all the way around) so that you can take a proper measurement of the gauge through the middle of the swatch:

Tension

Tension within a knitted piece means how tightly or loosely you have worked the stitches:

- If you knit too tightly, your gauge will have too many stitches for the block size given

- If you knit too loosely, your gauge will have too few stitches for the block size given

Blocking

Blocking your finished pieces (i.e. the sleeves to make up the sweater or the separately colored squares to make up a blanket) means that you end up working with the same size pieces when putting it all together – two sleeves which match or 36 squares which match.

Two forms of blocking will be covered in this section:

- Spray blocking
- Wet blocking

Spray blocking

This method uses a spray bottle to wet the knitted piece down when blocking. Here are the steps you should use when spray blocking:

- Use a blocking board to secure the knitted piece

- Lay the piece wrong side up if you have used a basic, flat stitch (or right-side up if you have used textured stitches)

- Line up the knitted piece on the blocking board and measure out

- Pin the edges carefully (making sure to use rustproof pins)

- Spray the item until it is fully wet (make sure that the water within the spray bottle is at room temperature – too hot and the knitted piece will shrink)

- Press down gently to create an overall flatness and evenness

- Allow the piece to dry

- Remove it from the blocking board

If you need to block several items, either ensure you have a board big enough to accommodate them or purchase several blocking boards.

Wet blocking

This method involves saturating the knitted piece before blocking. Here are the steps you should use when wet blocking:

- Completely immerse the knitted piece in a sink (or tub) full of water (room temperature)

- Lay the wet item on a towel and fold the ends of the towel over the item gently

- Roll the towel to remove the majority of the water (without squeezing or folding)

- Remove the item from the towel and block as given for *"**Spray blocking**"*

Lesson #10 – Unraveling

Unraveling is probably the biggest grumble amongst knitters and here's why. If you are someone who loves to crochet, each stitch you make is secured by the stitch previously made. You can remove the hook and the work stays put so long as you don't pull on the left over end of yarn.

With knitting, however, if a stitch is dropped accidentally, you will soon find that the knitted piece starts unraveling quite quickly. For a novice knitter, this spells disaster and many a knitted piece has been intentionally unraveled as a result in order to start all over again.

Want to know the secret? Have a crochet hook to hand to help you pick up those dropped stitches. Here's how:

- If possible, catch the dropped stitch quickly (within 2 or 3 rows if you can) – this is because you need enough flexibility to work the dropped stitch back up to the surface – if you discover it too many rows down, the knitted piece will have tightened around it making it impossible for you to work it back in (if this happens, it is best to unravel your work back down to the dropped stitch and reknit the unraveled rows).

- Once you have found your dropped stitch, use a crochet hook and turn your work so that the RS faces you (the knit side).

- Insert the crochet hook (from the front) into the dropped stitch and, while pointing the hook upwards, catch the horizontal strand from the row above and pull it through the dropped stitch.

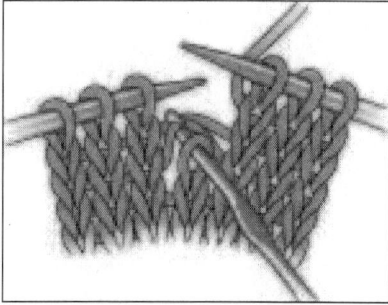

- Repeat this step until you are back to the top of your knitted piece.

- Replace the dropped stitch onto the holding needle (be careful it doesn't get twisted) and knit the stitch as normal.

Note: If you find more than one dropped stitch, use stitch markers to hold them all in place and work them back in – one at a time.

Lesson #11 – Other Stitches (Double Moss, Raindrops, Shell Stitch)

As you will learn during your time in the wonderful world of knitting, the types of stitches you can create is endless. People are always coming up with new ones to tempt you.

However, if you feel you have a firm grasp of the basics and want to delve just a bit further in your knowledge, try some (or indeed all) of the ones below. They are fantastic for texture and variety in your finished piece.

- Knotted Openwork
- Double Moss
- Raindrops
- Miniature Shell Stitch

Knotted Openwork

To create the knotted openwork stitch:

- Cast on the required number of stitches (to make a swatch, try 45 stitches)
- For Row 1, purl all stitches
- For Row 2, K2, * yarn over, K3, sl the 1st of these three knitted stitches over the other two, rep from * to the last stitch, K1
- For Row 3, purl all stitches
- For Row 4, K1, * K3, slip the 1st of these three knitted stitches over the other two, yarn over; rep from * to last two stitches, k2.
- Repeat these four rows until you have the desired length

Your finished piece should look something like:

Double Moss

This is one of the easiest patterns to follow but you have to pay attention to which row you are on for the pattern to work correctly.

- Cast on the required number of stitches (to make a swatch, try 44 stitches)
- For Row 1, K1, P1 and repeat until the end
- For Row 2 (and all subsequent **even** rows), knit the knit stitches and purl the purl stitches
- For Row 3 (and all subsequent **odd** rows), knit the purl stitches and purl the knit stitches
- Repeat the instructions for odd and even rows until you have the desired length

Your finished piece should look something like:

Raindrops

This is a beautiful stitch for a blanket or afghan and well worth a try:

- Cast on the required number of stitches (to make a swatch, try 45 stitches)
- For Row 1, K1, * insert the working needle in between next two stitches on holding needle, pull the yarn through and onto the working needle, K2tog, rep from * to end
- For Row 2, purl all stitches
- Repeat these two rows until you have the desired length

Your finished piece should look something like:

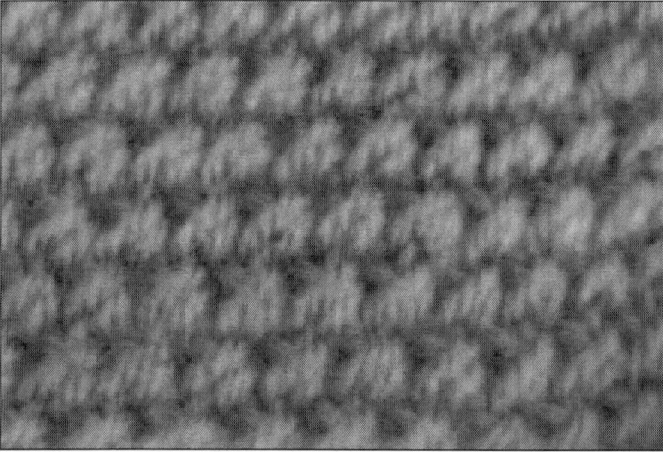

Miniature Shell Stitch

Shell stitches are perfect for making garments for little girls or for making baby blankets – here's how:

- Cast on the required number of stitches (to make a swatch, try 51 stitches)
- For Row 1, knit all stitches
- For Row 2, purl all stitches
- For Row 3, K2, * yarn over, P1, P3tog, P1, yarn over, K2, rep from * to end
- For Row 4, purl all stitches
- Repeat these four rows until you have the desired length

Your finished piece should look something like:

Conclusion

I'd like to thank you for joining me in this adventure of learning a new craft and entering the world of knitting? Isn't it great to wake the brain up and learn something new?

I hope that the steps, diagrams and advice given in this book have helped to teach you something new and, if you already knew the basics, then I hope it cemented your foundation knowledge enough to move onto bigger and better projects.

It could be that you have finally found a way of regaining your peace of mind and taking that time out to relax while still learning something new.

As for me, even though I consider myself an old hand when it comes to knitting, there were a few things that I needed to improve on as well – and I did!

I hope that somewhere along the way you found one or more techniques useful, and I hope all the advice given has helped you to understand the difference between American and British terminology as well as some creative ideas for your next new piece.

Now that you know the basics, there's no reason why you can't create your own new designs – all you need is some imagination, some graph paper and a pencil!

I'm confident that if you practice the steps given in this book, you will undoubtedly learn everything you need to know to create that new baby outfit or blanket. Who knows where this newfound knowledge will take you?

Above all else, remember that these steps can be learned, practiced and repeated numerous times to get the results you want. Yes, it will take time but you will get there – one small step at a time.

So roll up your sleeves, pick up your knitting needles and give it a go! What have you got to lose? It's up to you to apply the knowledge you now possess. Don't be afraid to try!

Don't be afraid to try a stitch in a different way or to hold the knitting needles differently – if it works for you, then go with it. The only limit to any knitted piece you make is your imagination.

If you like moss stitch, work with moss stitch. If you prefer the shell stitch, then use that. Try combining the two – the result could be quite remarkable.

You may also find that once your newfound talent is discovered, requests from family and friends will come rolling in. Cherish it – there's nothing more rewarding than making something for a loved one.

The biggest thing to remember? Believe and achieve!

I wish you the best of luck!

To your success,

Amy Taggart

Preview Of "Crochet For Beginners - The Ultimate Guide to Learn How to Crochet & Start Creating Beautiful Things (With Pictures!)"

Lesson #1 - Welcome To the Amazing World of Crochet!

Before we get fully started in the different types of stitches and how to read patterns, let's look at some of the topics which will help you secure a solid foundation in the world of crochet:

- What is crochet?
- Types of yarn
- Yarn labeling
- Hook types
- Hook sizes
- Left-handed
- Grip types

What is crochet?

For centuries, people have confused knitting with crochet and vice versa. To set the record straight, knitting usually involves two pointed, but straight needles which are used together to create a tightly woven piece which can al   so include a wide variety of textures. It is commonly used for garments.

The word **'crochet'** has its origin in France and it literally means **'hook'**. This means that crochet is completed with a hooked needle and involves the process of pulling loops of yarn (or other fibers) through other loops in order to create either tight or loose stitches with a wide variety of textures. Crochet is commonly used for the creation of afghans, bedspreads and other large items due to the speed with which the yarn can be worked.

Do bear in mind, however, that it doesn't matter whether you use knitting or crochet to create something – if you are happy with the needlecraft you use, that's fine. For the purposes of this book, however, we will be looking at crochet only.

It is also worth mentioning that there is no one right way or wrong way of working with a crochet hook – use whatever method works for you in order to obtain the right tension and gauge for your end project.

Types of yarn

There are several different types of yarn which can be used when crocheting and the type you choose will normally be in direct relation to the type of item you are creating. Several of these types will be discussed in more detail in the following subsections such as double knit, worsted weight and baby yarn.

You will also find types of yarn which won't be covered in this book, but as your knowledge and skill increases, you can try your hand at. These include yarn such as coned yarn, kitchen cotton and eyelash yarn as well as specialty varieties such as ruffle or lace yarn.

Labeling systems on yarn packaging has been created by the Craft Yarn Council to ensure uniformity to the yarn being supplied to the crafter. Please note that not all manufacturers use this system; however, the vast majority does.

The main thing to remember is to practice with a smooth yarn which works through your fingers easily. This is imperative until you learn how to get the correct gauge and tension.

Double knit

Double knit yarn (also known as DK weight) is one of the most popular weights of yarn for both knitting and crochet. It is ideal for light-weight projects and can be used for baby garments and blankets if it is soft enough.

It falls within the number '**3**' area of weighted yarns (or '**Light**') by the Craft Yarn Council – look for the following when purchasing DK yarn:

Some of the most popular brands of DK yarn include a portion of the LB Collection, Merino and Microspun.

Worsted weight

Worsted weight yarn is what is known as a yarn which is somewhat heavier than double knit (or DK) as well as yarns like sport weight, crochet thread, fingering weight, and baby weight yarn. However, it is considered to be lighter than bulky or chunky yarn.

It is an ideal yarn for the creation of toys, accessories, clothing and afghans and blankets.

Labels for worsted weight yarn usually show the number '**4**' somewhere on the label to indicate that it is of medium weight. You may also see the word '**Medium**' on the label to confirm this:

MEDIUM

Some of the most popular brands of worsted weight yarns include Bernat, Lion Brand, Coats and Clark, and Red Heart.

Baby Yarn

Baby yarn is one of the finest yarns you can buy and is perfect for creating baby garments, blankets and afghans (as its name implies).

It comes under both '1' and '2' area of weighted yarns by the Craft Yarn Council where '1' is known as 'Super Fine' and '2' is known as 'Fine' – look for the following when purchasing baby yarn:

Some of the most popular brands of baby yarns include a portion of the LB collection, Sock-Ease and Bonbons.

Yarn labels

We have briefly touched on one portion of the yarn label but in order to know what you are working with when it comes to the various fibers available, here are a few more helpful tips about the information shown on your yarn label:

- **Care instructions** – this portion of the label will help you care for the finished product and how you should go about washing and drying the crocheted piece. If you are using a very delicate yarn, you may need to opt for hand washing or dry cleaning to care for it.

- **Color name** – Each ball of yarn is given a name which normally closely refers to the color of the yarn itself.

- **Color / dye lot number** – Each ball of yarn should also have a number shown on the label which refers to its dye lot. A dye lot refers to the batch of yarn created when it was dyed. This is particularly useful when you run out of a color – you can use the combination of brand, name and dye lot number to order more. Be careful when ordering more yarn of a certain color as different dye lots can have result in slightly different shades.

- **Yarn ply** – This information will tell you the number of strands contained in the yarn (i.e. how many strands have been twisted together to make the single strand of yarn). You will see things like 2-ply, 4-ply or perhaps even 12-ply. Keep in mind that the ply number does not indicate weight or thickness of the yarn – it is possible to have a chunky 2-ply yarn and a very delicate 12-ply yarn.

- **Recommended hook** – many yarn labels will give you an indication of the size hook which is best suited to the yarn. By sticking to the suggestion given, you should be able to obtain the correct gauge.

- **Yards** – The label will, more than likely, tell you how many yards of yarn are contained within any given ball. Make sure to pay attention to this as a chunky yarn will have less yardage than a fine baby yarn.

There are many other bits of information which can be shown on a yarn label, but you should at least have enough to get you started.

The crochet hook

Crochet hooks are also known as crochet needles, although this term can be misleading as a needle normally has an eye – crochet hooks do not. We will be using the term '**hook**' or '**crochet hook**' throughout this book to prevent any confusion.

Crochet hooks have a hook at one end (as the name implies) and there are some which have a hook at both ends while others still may have a stopper at one end.

For the purposes of learning basic crochet, you will need a crochet hook with a hook at one end only. Samples of these are shown below:

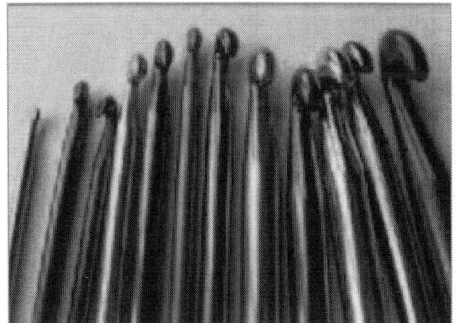

In order to understand the basics of crochet, it is important to learn why a crochet hook is made the way it is. It may look like it is just a straight piece of metal (or wood or even bamboo) with a hook on the end but, in reality; each crochet hook is made up of five separate areas:

- The handle
- The thumb rest
- The shaft
- The throat
- The point

Each of these will now be looked at in a bit more detail. So that you know what is being discussed, a diagram of a crochet hook is given below:

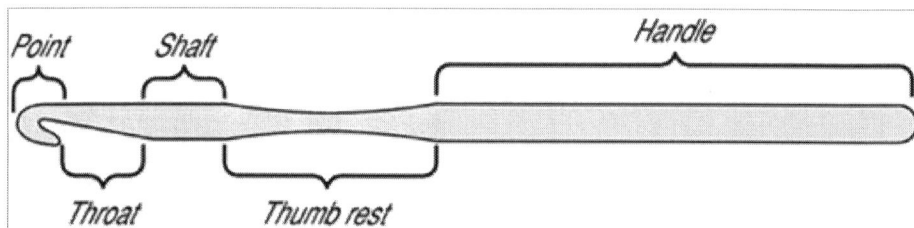

The handle

The handle's sole purpose is to ensure that you retain balance while crocheting. If the handle is too short, you will end up dropping the crochet hook on a regular basis due to the sheer amount of work you are doing at the other end of the hook.

The thumb rest

The thumb rest portion of the crochet hook should be held between your middle finger and your thumb – this allows you to have maximum rotation of the hook for working each stitch. However, don't worry if you hold yours slightly differently.

The shaft

The shaft portion of the crochet hook is where all the hooked stitches reside until they are pulled back off of the hook as part of the next stitch (or set of stitches). It is this part of the hook which tends to determine your tension.

The throat

The throat portion of the crochet hook is used for grabbing the yarn as you work. It is important that the throat is small enough to prevent loops from sliding off of the hook but also large enough to work with chunkier yarns.

The point

The point of the crochet hook is inserted into the previously made stitches in order to create your next stitch. A good point should be blunt enough to avoid splitting your yarn but sharp enough to glide through each stitch.

Experiment with different types of crochet hooks until you find a brand which works fluidly for you. It should be easy to hold and easy to work with while still providing you a consistent tension and gauge.

Hook sizes

Crochet hooks come in a wide range of sizes and, depending on the country in which you reside; you will need to know which size needle to look for. The list below will provide you with a quick list:

To check out the rest of "Crochet For Beginners - The Ultimate Guide to Learn How to Crochet & Start Creating Beautiful Things (With Pictures!) go to Amazon right now!

10485444R00051

Printed in Great Britain
by Amazon.co.uk, Ltd.,
Marston Gate.